Albert Einstein

I have an idea!
E=mc²
I have an idea!

Albert Einstein

by Wil Mara

Illustrated by Charlotte Ager

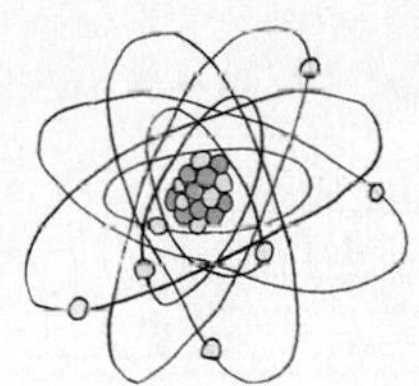

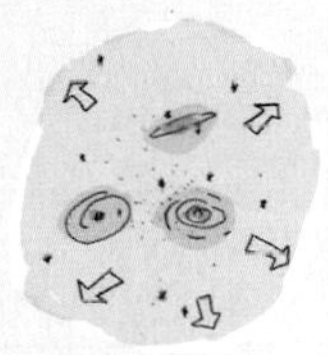

Senior Editor Shannon Beatty
Senior Designer Joanne Clark

Project Editor Roohi Sehgal
Additional Editorial Kritika Gupta
Project Art Editor Yamini Panwar
Jacket Coordinator Francesca Young
Jacket Designer Joanne Clark
DTP Designers Sachin Gupta, Vijay Kandwal
Picture Researcher Aditya Katyal
Illustrator Charlotte Ager
Pre-Producer Nadine King
Producer Basia Ossowska
Managing Editors Laura Gilbert, Monica Saigal
Deputy Managing Art Editor Ivy Sengupta
Managing Art Editor Diane Peyton Jones
Delhi Team Head Malavika Talukder
Creative Director Helen Senior
Publishing Director Sarah Larter

Subject Consultant Eve Mandel
Literacy Consultant Stephanie Laird
Physics Consultant Jose Lazar Vargas

First American Edition, 2019
Published in the United States by DK Publishing
345 Hudson Street, New York, New York 10014

19 20 21 22 23 10 9 8 7 6 5 4 3 2 1
001–308812–Jan/19

Published in Great Britain by Dorling Kindersley Limited

A catalog record for this book is available from the Library of Congress.
ISBN: 978-1-4654-7570-1 (Paperback)
ISBN: 978-1-4654-7443-8 (Hardcover)

Printed and bound in China

Dear Reader,

Ever wonder how to change the world? Simple—you get a few ideas that you know to be good ones, and you follow them through.

That might just be the story of Albert Einstein's life. His ideas were the product of a mind that comes along perhaps once every century. But it took more than ideas for him to change the way we look at the universe. It also took drive, determination, focus, and a refusal to "give in" and do what everyone else does.

Albert was a freethinker. He knew some people wouldn't agree with his ideas. It's always scary when people challenge the beliefs you've held for so long. But Albert cared about getting down to the truth of things. He wanted humankind to get things right. He once spoke of " . . . the understanding of that which is truly significant."

Luckily for us, it was this understanding that he spent his life pursuing.

Wil Mara

The life of... Albert Einstein

1
SMART FROM THE START
page 8

5
THE ACADEMIC
page 50

6
A HOUSEHOLD NAME
page 62

7
A MAN WITHOUT A COUNTRY
page 74

8
ALBERT THE AMERICAN
page 84

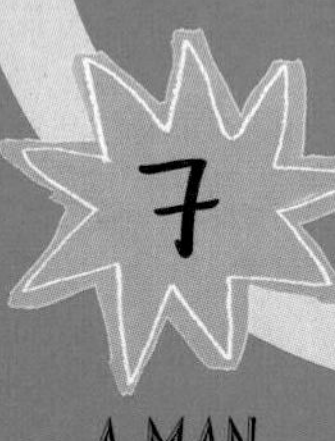

2
SCHOOL DAYS
page 18
3
THE PATENT CLERK
page 30
4
THE MIRACLE YEAR
page 40
9
THE MANHATTAN PROJECT
page 92
10
FINAL YEARS
page 102

Chapter 1

Smart FROM THE start

Albert Einstein is considered one of the most brilliant people in history, and there were signs of his genius from the earliest days of his life.

Albert was born into a family that already had its fair share of smart people. His father, Hermann, had been an excellent student with a particular gift for mathematics. Only his parents' money problems kept him from going on to higher education, or college. In early adulthood, Hermann and a cousin became owners of a company that made beds. After that, Hermann and his brother, Jakob, started a business that provided gas and electrical supplies.

Albert's mother, Pauline, came from a very successful family. Her father made a fortune selling grain. Pauline went to good schools and

was a model student. She was well-educated, which was fairly unusual for a woman at that time. She also had a great sense of humor and loved the arts, particularly music.

Albert, Hermann and Pauline's first child, was born on March 14, 1879, in the southern German town of Ulm. Right from the start, there was something very different about him. He rarely spoke for the first few years of his life, whereas most children begin to talk by about the age of two.

Albert's parents, Hermann and Pauline Einstein. Hermann was excellent at math, while Pauline had a gift for the arts.

When Albert finally began to talk, he had a strange habit of speaking his sentences very softly, over and over, to himself. It was as if he was trying them out before he let anyone else hear them. This habit troubled some of the people around him. The woman that the Einsteins hired as a maid even called him the "Dopey One." However, she and many others would soon discover that little Albert was about as far from dopey as anyone could be.

One of the most important moments in Albert's childhood happened when he was about five. He became ill and had to stay in bed for a time. While there, his father gave him a compass as a gift.

Young Albert was utterly fascinated by this. He was enthralled by the fact that the compass's needle was reacting to an invisible force rather than some other object touching or moving it. And it wasn't enough that he was fascinated by it—he wanted to know *how* it happened, and *why* it happened.

HOW A COMPASS WORKS

A compass is a very simple device—a magnet shaped like a needle, spinning freely, with one end that always points toward the Earth's magnetic North Pole. This happens because the Earth has a magnetic field, and the northern side of it draws one end of all magnets in its direction.

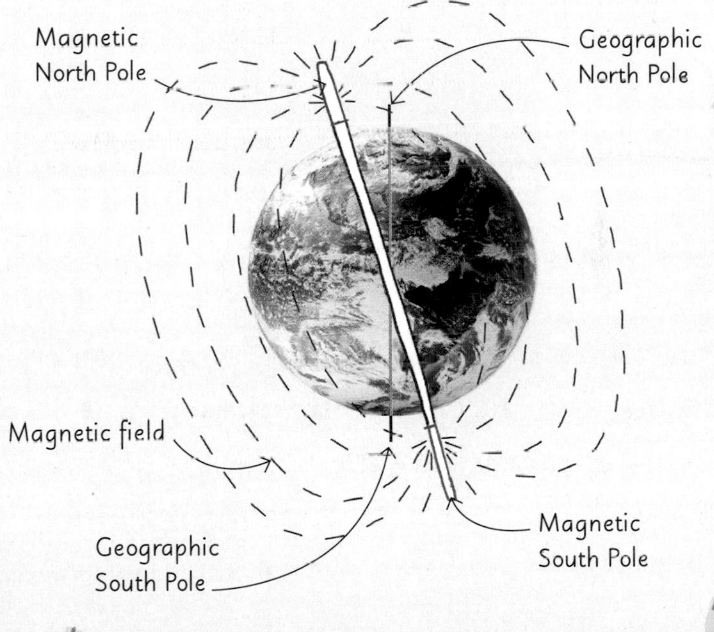

Many years later, he would say of the incident that this ". . . experience made a deep and lasting impression," and concluded that, "Something deeply hidden had to be behind things." In fact, it was this very attitude that guided him toward a career in the sciences. Whereas most people simply accepted things like magnetism and gravity and other invisible forces, Albert sought to understand what made them work.

One of the challenges Albert faced because of his unusual way of thinking was that it made him different from others his age. While most boys would spend a sunny afternoon outside playing ball, Albert would sit and wonder about all sorts of things. He would try to carry out scientific experiments in his head, seeing them clearly as images rather than in terms of words or ideas. For example, he thought about how gravity's effect on him would change if he was standing inside an elevator that was rapidly falling. He would wonder, "Would I still be affected by gravity and would I still be standing on the elevator floor? What would be holding me there?"

What is gravity? A force that makes objects fall toward the Earth rather than away from it. It is gravity that gives weight to all matter.

"I have no special talent. I am only passionately curious."

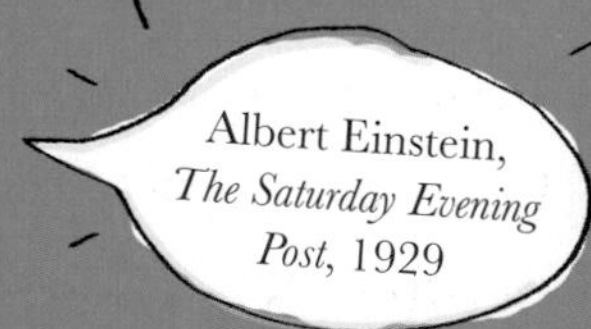

Albert also spent hours by himself playing with his favorite toys. One was a set of building blocks, from which he would make complex and unusual structures. He also had a small engine powered by steam that he received from an uncle. He would watch the engine work and then try to figure out the scientific principles behind it. It was all part of a powerful curiosity he had about the world and how it worked. This would be the driving force throughout his life.

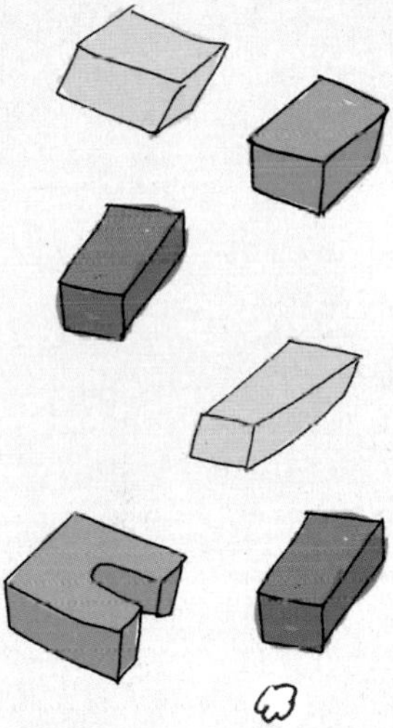

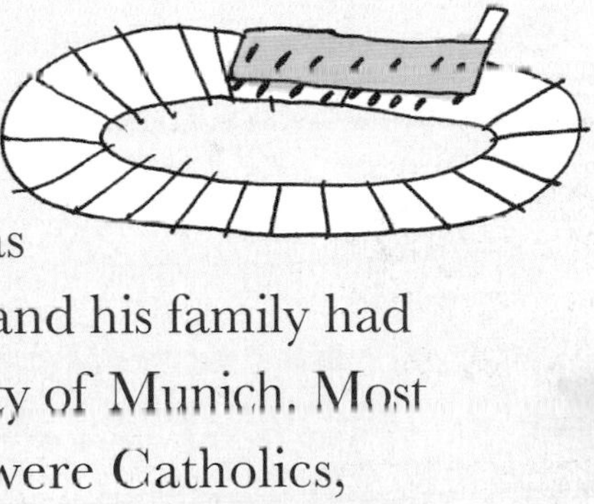

By the time Albert was ready to start school, he and his family had moved to the German city of Munich. Most of the people in Munich were Catholics, whereas the Einsteins were Jewish. Albert's parents were not particularly religious, but Albert was still teased by the other children for being different. This made him feel lonely, but it also helped him to look at the world differently. He became determined to uncover the secrets behind the invisible forces of life. Albert soon developed into a very independent boy who wasn't afraid to question anyone or anything.

DID YOU KNOW?

Albert's birthday is also Pi Day—March 14, or 3.14, for pi! 3.14 is a special number in math and science.

As his first year of school approached, young Albert was more than ready. The real question was whether or not the schools in Munich were ready for him!

Albert had one sibling—his younger sister Maria, nicknamed, "Maja." She was often his only friend during his otherwise lonely childhood.

Chapter 2

School days

Albert's school days were interesting. Sometimes he was a model student—and other times he would drive his teachers crazy!

Albert began attending school in 1885, when he was six years old. This was the age at which all children were required to begin their education in Munich. His parents enrolled him in a school called Petersschule, which was close to where the Einsteins lived.

Petersschule may have seemed like an unusual choice because it was primarily a Catholic school and Albert was the only Jewish boy in his grade. He was sometimes bullied by his classmates for this, which likely made him feel more isolated than ever.

Petersschule, however, was also known for its high academic standards, and Albert's parents wanted to make sure their son got a good education. He turned out to be an excellent student, often earning higher marks than anyone else. However, he did not care for the rigid way the school was run. Children were expected to be as obedient as soldiers, which simply did not fit with Albert's way of thinking. Nevertheless, he kept quiet and generally stayed out of trouble.

In 1888, after three years at Petersschule, Albert began attending another Munich school—Luitpold Gymnasium. He took many different courses and again earned good grades. He was not particularly fond of all his classes, though. He did not have a great interest in Greek and Latin, for example. He did, however, enjoy receiving instruction on the Hebrew language and the Jewish faith in general. He eventually began to study Christianity and read the Bible as well.

DID YOU KNOW?

At the time in Germany, the word "gymnasium" didn't mean a place where students had gym class, but rather a school that prepared students for college.

His favorite classes were those involving mathematics and science. He would learn about the branch of science called physics when he was a little bit older. Through his theories in physics, Albert would make his mark on history.

What is physics? The study of physical things, what happens when they move around, and why they move the way they do.

He also spent a lot of his free time studying math and science. This not only put him well ahead of his fellow students but sometimes ahead of his teachers! By the time he was just 14 years old, he had a firm understanding of calculus—an advanced form of mathematics that most people never grasp in their lifetime.

REBEL WITHOUT A SOCK

Albert was known throughout his life for his quirky ways, and one of his most famous was his unwillingness to wear socks. He once explained to a friend that this habit began when he was still very young, and his big toes used to break through whatever socks he had on at the time. So, he decided there was no point in wearing them at all! He carried this habit well into adulthood, going so far as to "go sockless" even when in the company of royalty! In such situations, he enjoyed the fact that he was engaging in a small act of rebellion—yet one that went unnoticed by everyone but him.

The Einstein family suffered a major setback in 1894 when the company owned by Albert's father filed for bankruptcy. Albert's parents responded to this misfortune in a somewhat unusual way—they moved to Italy, but they left Albert behind! They insisted that he finish his education at Luitpold, and they set him up in a boardinghouse. (A boardinghouse is a temporary home that also provides meals for the people who are staying there.) Albert continued his studies, but the whole experience of being alone made him deeply unhappy.

What is bankruptcy?

When people or organizations lose all their money. If people file for bankruptcy, it means they can no longer pay back any money they might owe to others.

He was also facing the possibility of being forced into the military, which was something he did not want to do. So, Albert left Munich later that year without properly graduating from Luitpold Gymnasium—to rejoin his family in Italy.

Albert's parents were very upset, but Albert had no intention of returning to Luitpold. Instead, he wanted to go to the Swiss Federal Polytechnic School, also known as the Zurich Polytechnic. This was basically a college-level institution, yet Albert didn't even have what amounted to a high school diploma. Still, he was allowed to take the entrance exams, which were very difficult. His scores in math and physics were exceptional. Swiss Federal still wanted Albert to attend, but only under the condition that he finish up his earlier courses.

DID YOU KNOW?

Albert was brilliant with the math and physics parts of the Polytechnic entrance exam—but the rest of it, not so much!

Jost Winteler taught young Albert history and Greek.

Albert did this by enrolling in a secondary school in Aarau, Switzerland. During this time, he was allowed to stay at the home of one of the school's teachers, Jost Winteler, and he got along very well with the entire Winteler family. It was one of the happiest times of Albert's childhood. When he completed his studies in Aarau, he returned to his own family feeling more positive and upbeat than he had in years.

Albert enrolled in the Swiss Federal Polytechnic School in the fall of 1896. In spite of his time spent in Aarau, he still wasn't really qualified to attend—he was only 17, and you had to be 18 to be accepted into Swiss Federal. But they accepted him anyway because it had become clear by this point that Albert had a very special mind.

Another important event in Albert's life that occurred in 1896 was that he gave up his German citizenship. In spite of his young age, Albert had already come to believe that violence and warfare were the wrong ways to go about resolving conflicts. He had left Munich and the Luitpold Gymnasium in part because he was afraid of being drafted. Germany was becoming more aggressive at the time, and even more so by

Albert was only 17 when he enrolled in the Swiss Federal Polytechnic School.

the late 1890s. Albert was afraid that, even though he was no longer living in Germany, he would still be called back for military duty. So, with his parents' approval, he gave up his German citizenship. Albert's pacifism would be an important feature of his personality throughout the rest of his life: In later life, Albert would call himself a "militant pacifist."

Albert's main ambition at the Swiss Federal Polytechnic School was to earn a teaching degree. He certainly had the brains for it, and his gentle, humorous nature would undoubtedly have made him popular with his future students. And yet, Albert made this dream more difficult by being a somewhat poor student himself!

For example, Albert skipped many classes during his years at Swiss Federal.

DID YOU KNOW?

Albert was stateless for nearly five years before he became a Swiss citizen in 1901.

What is pacifism? The belief that war and violence are never justified. Pacifism argues for peaceful resolutions to conflicts.

MUSICALLY MINDED

Albert's mother, Pauline, passed her love of music to her son and taught him how to play both the piano and violin. As a teenager his interest in the violin greatly intensified, and he developed a love for classical music. He once wrote to a friend that Mozart's music was, "so pure that it seemed to have been ever-present in the universe, waiting to be discovered by the master." As an adult, he would often play in public. Unfortunately, no recordings of any of these performances are known to exist.

Instead, he often studied the notes taken in class by friends. One of the main reasons Albert rebelled was because he still had a deep dislike for authority, and several of his professors were quite strict and inflexible.

Albert also didn't like the way certain mathematical and scientific subjects were taught. Again, it was a case of him believing he knew more than his teachers. He knew this would make him unpopular with his instructors, but he was not willing to bend.

Albert often read books on his own when he was supposed to be in class. These books were more advanced than those recommended by the school. In this sense, he really did receive a tremendous education, absorbing works by leaders in the fields of math and physics, as well as other subjects that interested him, such as philosophy. When it came time for Albert to take his formal exams, his scores were outstanding. He eventually graduated with the degree he so desperately wanted—but his defiant behavior would have a lasting effect that made the next stage of his life very difficult indeed.

"I am not only a pacifist but a **militant pacifist.** I am willing to **fight for peace.** Nothing will end war unless the people themselves **refuse to go to war.**"

Albert Einstein, in a 1931 interview

Chapter 3

THE patent clerk

Albert had dreams of greatness after finishing school. But he would soon learn that the road to the future can sometimes be very bumpy!

Albert graduated from the Zurich Polytechnic in August 1900. Sticking with his plans of becoming a teacher, he first needed to get some experience as a teacher's assistant. This, however, would not be as easy as he imagined.

He had been fairly rebellious and stubborn when he was a student at the Polytechnic. As a result, some of his professors disliked him—yet he needed some of those same professors to recommend him for an assistant's job after graduation.

Albert first tried for a position at the Polytechnic itself, but no one was willing to take a chance on him. They did need to hire some assistants, but they refused to consider someone they viewed as unpredictable.

Albert responded to this with a letter-writing campaign to other schools, but he kept running into the same problem. Anyone who thought about hiring him eventually contacted his former professors at the Polytechnic, and Albert would be turned down shortly thereafter.

After about two frustrating years of job hunting, Albert was forced to accept a position as patent clerk in the Swiss city of Bern.

WHAT'S A PATENT CLERK?

A patent clerk reviews applications for new inventions and determines whether or not they should be granted official patents, or copyrights. Part of this work includes making sure proposed inventions aren't too close in design and purpose to those that are already patented. Another part is making sure the new inventions work the way they're supposed to.

The problem with this kind of work was that it was too easy for him. Albert had a brilliant mind, and he quickly became bored. He would do his daily duties in half the time it took most of the other clerks. In a funny twist, his employer took this to mean he was really enthusiastic about the job, and he got a raise! While Albert was hardly enthusiastic, his fast pace at the patent office did mean he had more time to work on his theories about physics.

The young scientist indulged in his love of physics during his free time by gathering a group of friends together who shared the same interest. They called themselves the "Olympia Academy" (or *Akademie Olympia* in German) as a kind of joke, referring to the mythical Greek gods of Mount Olympus.

What is Mount Olympus?

The highest mountain in Greece, where the ancient Greeks believed the 12 most powerful gods lived.

The Olympia Academy is in session! Albert (far right) with Habicht and Solovine, the other main members of the group.

The Olympia Academy started when Albert put an ad in the paper offering his services as a math and physics tutor. One of the first people who contacted him was Maurice Solovine, who was actually a student of philosophy rather than math or physics; another was Conrad Habicht, a mathematician. There were a few other people as well, but these three men formed the core of the group.

They would meet at Albert's apartment, where discussions started with math and physics. Soon talks expanded to cover other things. Maurice Solovine, for example, introduced many philosophical topics, which Albert found fascinating. The Olympia Academy lasted for only two years, since Habicht and Solovine had both moved out of Bern by 1905. But the three men would remain friends for the rest of their lives. Perhaps more importantly, Albert claimed in the years ahead that his discussions with the Academy helped to form many of the ideas that would lead him to change the world.

Another important development in Albert's life as a scientist was that, around this time, he began to write and publish scientific papers.

Scientific papers can be thought of as "academic articles," since scholars write them in order to introduce new ideas in a particular subject.

Albert's first paper was called "Conclusions Drawn from the Capillarity Phenomena." It was published in 1901 in a German-language journal called *Annalen der Physik* (*Annals of Physics* in English). This paper described some of his ideas about the forces between molecules, especially how far molecules were from one another. Although his theories in this area would later turn out to be incorrect, the paper's publication marked a very important moment in Albert's personal history. It was his first contribution to the world of formal physics.

What are molecules? The smallest physical unit of a material. Molecules are groups of atoms that are held together by a naturally strong attraction between them.

A major moment in Albert's personal life came in 1903 when he got married. His new wife was a Serbian woman named Mileva Marić. She and Albert first met back in 1896 when they were both new students at the Zurich Polytechnic. They were little more than friends early on, but a romance blossomed when they began studying together outside of school.

Albert's wife, "Mileva," was very good at math.

Mileva had a bright mind, and she looked forward to a career not only as a teacher, but also as a contributor in the field of physics, just like Albert. However, their relationship took some unexpected turns that made this very challenging

DID YOU KNOW?

In 1896, Mileva was the only female enrolled at the Polytechnic for the purpose of getting a teaching certificate in math.

for her. In early 1902, Mileva gave birth to a daughter named Lieserl, and this forced her to set her career plans aside. Little is known of what became of Lieserl after this, but Einstein biographers believe she either died or was given up for adoption the following year. Albert would go on to have two more children with Mileva—Hans in 1904, and Eduard in 1910.

Mileva with her sons, Hans (right) and Eduard (left).

"Science can only be created by those who are thoroughly imbued with the aspiration toward truth and understanding."

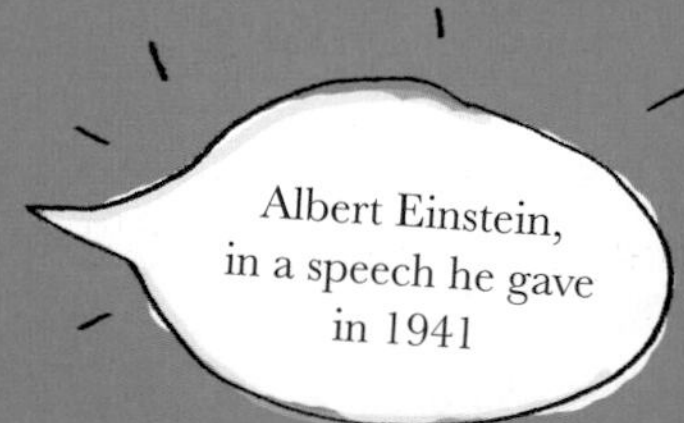

Albert and Mileva continued working together on their shared interest in physics, and continued supporting each other's goals. Albert kept writing for *Annalen der Physik*, mostly in the area of thermodynamics, which explores the relationship between heat and mechanical energy.

Albert believed that "Science can only be created by those . . . with the aspiration toward truth and understanding." Then came 1905—the year in which Albert would make his first big contribution to science. He would publish four scientific papers that would not only change his life, but also forever change the way we view the world around us.

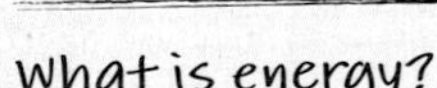

Stored ability to do work. For example, there is energy stored in food. When we eat, that energy moves to us.

Chapter 4

THE miracle year

Great scientists often make their mark on history over the course of many years. Albert changed the world of physics in just one.

As 1905 began, Albert found himself still without a teaching position, and still laboring away at the Bern patent office. But this would be an important year for the young scientist. Albert was in his mid-twenties, married, and caring for a son. He was also continuing to devote much of his free time to his tireless interest in physics. He had written several papers for the *Annalen der Physik* by this point, but none were considered

Albert with his wife Mileva and their newborn son, Hans Albert, in Zurich in 1904.

groundbreaking. Because of this, his work had not earned a lot of attention or praise. That, however, was about to change very quickly.

Albert had begun to doubt some of the oldest theories of physics—theories that had been accepted as fact for centuries. Since he was always eager to question things, he began forming theories of his own. He didn't just come up with his own theories to be a rebel—he did it because of his ongoing observations of the world around him. Albert did not have all the books and articles that were available on physics to help him with his ideas. He did, however, have a good friend named Michele Angelo Besso.

MICHELE ANGELO BESSO

Michele Angelo Besso (1873–1955) and Albert stayed close friends throughout their lives. When Besso died, Albert wrote a letter to his family expressing his sympathy.

Michele and Albert had been at the Zurich Polytechnic together, and then they worked together at the patent office. (Albert, in fact, helped him get the job!) Michele had an excellent understanding of physics and was happy to discuss it at great length with his friend. Albert called Michele "the best sounding board in Europe," when it came to physics. He even gave some suggestions that Albert later claimed to be very helpful.

Once Albert had his theories together, he was ready to share them with the world through four separate papers—and make history at the same time.

The first of Albert's four groundbreaking papers was published in *Annalen der Physik* on June 9. This paper discussed a way in

1905 was an important year for Albert's career in physics. He was 26 at the time.

which light behaves called the "photoelectric effect." At the time, it was thought that light always moved in continuous waves. Albert believed that although this was true most of the time, there were conditions under which light changed instead into disconnected particles. These particles would become known as photons, which were never still, but always moving.

WHAT ARE WAVES?

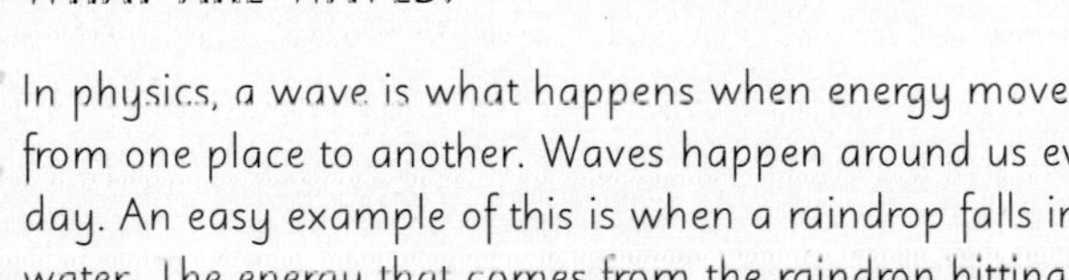
In physics, a wave is what happens when energy moves from one place to another. Waves happen around us every day. An easy example of this is when a raindrop falls into water. The energy that comes from the raindrop hitting the water causes waves.

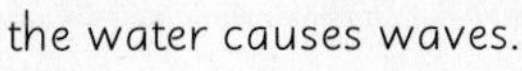

The second of Albert's papers was published just a little over a month later on July 18. It discussed the way particles move within different situations that surround them, such as a dust particle within a ray of light. When Albert observed particles moving in places where they should have been still, he concluded that tinier particles—atoms—were acting upon them.

Albert's third paper, published on September 26, offered revolutionary ideas about the relationship between space and time.

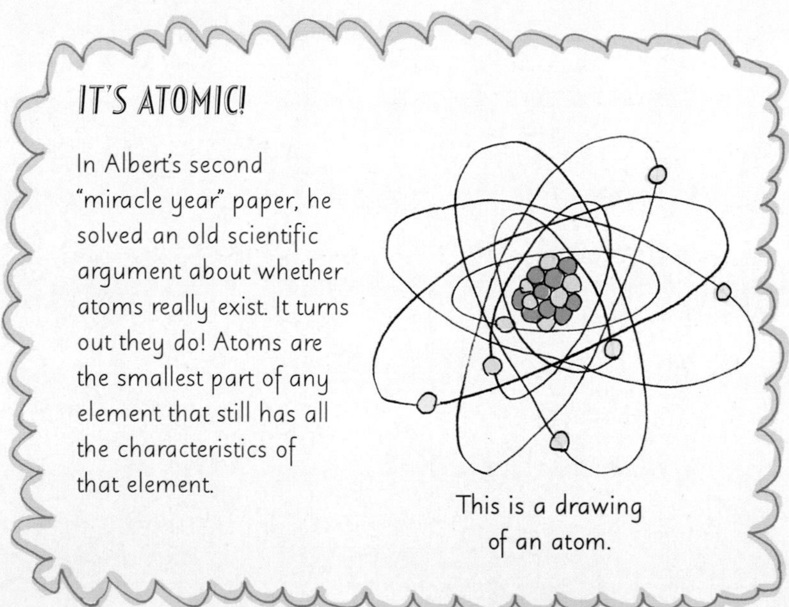

IT'S ATOMIC!

In Albert's second "miracle year" paper, he solved an old scientific argument about whether atoms really exist. It turns out they do! Atoms are the smallest part of any element that still has all the characteristics of that element.

This is a drawing of an atom.

A very important one was that the laws of physics still work the same way on an object even if that object is inside something that is moving. For example, if you are in a bus and throw a ball straight up in the air, that ball will come back down in your hand even though the bus is moving. This third paper introduced the world to what became known as Albert's "Theory of Special Relativity."

The fourth of Albert's "miracle year" papers was published on November 21. In this paper, Albert discussed the amount of energy that was inside any object. There were two parts to this. The first part was kinetic energy, which is how much energy an object has when it is moving. The second part was rest energy, which is how much energy an object has when it isn't moving. The ideas in this paper introduced the world to Albert's most well-known equation: $E=mc^2$.

Not long after each of Albert's four papers were published, some of the most influential physicists of the time took notice of their intriguing new theories. When they tested the theories themselves and proved Albert was right, he became the talk of the scientific world! Virtually no one had ever heard of this man, yet he had just altered basic principles that had been accepted as law for centuries.

One physicist named Jakob Johann Laub decided to get to know Albert, and find out who he was.

A MASSIVE CONCEPT

$E=mc^2$ is the equation for which Albert is most famous. In physics terms, this stands for "energy equals mass times the speed of light squared." Put simply, it says that energy and physical mass are really the same thing. Albert believed that mass comes from trapping energy, and when that energy is released, it moves at the speed of light. (That speed is incredible, by the way—light travels 186,000 miles / 300,000 km every second!) A well-known example of such energy being used was with the two atomic bombs that were dropped at the end of World War II. Millions upon millions of atoms were split open, instantly releasing massive amounts of energy.

A mushroom cloud forms when an atomic bomb explodes.

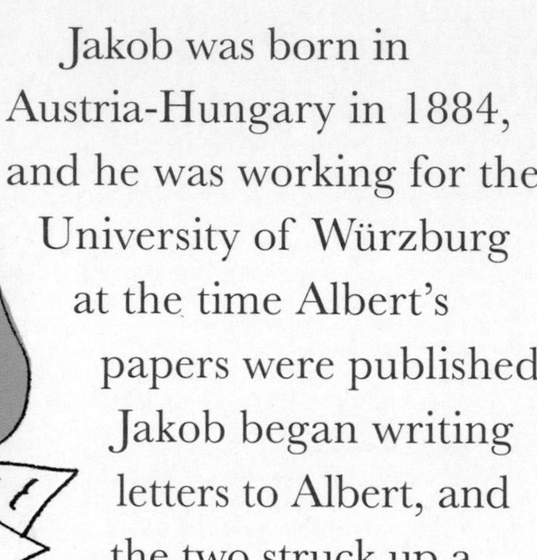

Jakob was born in Austria-Hungary in 1884, and he was working for the University of Würzburg at the time Albert's papers were published. Jakob began writing letters to Albert, and the two struck up a friendship. In 1908, Jakob decided to visit Albert in Bern. He was astonished to find Albert still in his patent-clerk job, and thought it was a waste of Albert's extraordinary talents. Albert still wanted a teaching position, but he felt that being a patent clerk had its advantages, too. His pay was good enough to support himself and his family, and he had enough spare time to continue his physics studies.

Albert and Jakob worked together to develop Albert's theories in regard to special relativity. The original theory covered the concept as relating only to one body at rest and another one at a constant speed. What he and Jakob began investigating was how special relativity applies to bodies moving at different speeds. Albert would work on this for years to come, making repeated attempts to find the fundamental answers behind it.

DID YOU KNOW?

Albert was very disorganized. He was so busy thinking about physics, that he often missed appointments.

In the meantime, as his reputation grew, he at last received the opportunity he'd craved for so long—to become an academic.

Chapter 5

The academic

Albert stayed at the patent office for a few more years after publishing his papers in 1905. That, however, was all about to change!

The scientific world would not allow such an extraordinary mind to remain in this kind of job for long. Academics were quickly realizing they had a once-in-a-generation genius on their hands, and they had to bring Albert into the world of academia, where he belonged—and as soon as possible!

1905 was an important year for Albert because he earned his doctorate and was thereafter known as "Dr. Einstein." To earn a doctorate, or PhD, a postgraduate student must write a doctoral dissertation, which is a formal essay. Albert, like any other student, needed his doctorate in order to find a good teaching post.

Albert's first teaching job finally came in 1908, when he was hired as an assistant at the University of Bern. This position marked the beginning of what would be a quick rise in the academic world. His job title was *privatdozent*, which meant he could teach students but was not part of the school's faculty. It also meant he did not receive a salary. Because of this, he had to keep his job at the patent office for the time being—it provided him with a steady paycheck. He also likely knew he

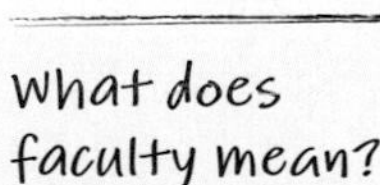

Refers mostly to the teachers of a particular school. Sometimes administrators are also included in this definition.

had to do this kind of assistant work before any school could make him a professor.

The ambitious scientist finally earned his professorship in mid 1909, at which time he said goodbye to his job as a patent clerk. He became an "associate professor" of theoretical physics, which was a new position created specifically for him at the University of Zurich.

This new job was a big step up from his *privatdozent* position in Bern, but it was not

The University of Zurich, where Albert got a job as a professor.

enough to put him among the top level of academics just yet. Albert still had to teach classes every week, and he still had to supervise other students. He wasn't particularly happy about this part of the job, since it took him away from his beloved research.

However, he didn't remain at the University of Zurich for very long. Albert was given a full professorship in 1911 at the Charles-Ferdinand University in Prague. Then he moved yet again, just a year later, taking a position at his old school, Zurich Polytechnic. He was at the Polytechnic from 1912 to 1914.

Albert focused his work particularly on proving some of his earlier theories. He was trying to figure out if his ideas applied to bodies that moved independently of one another.

Albert also studied aspects of thermodynamics and gravity. He was helped in this research by an old friend of his named Marcel Grossmann. Marcel was the fellow student at the Zurich Polytechnic who took notes during the lectures that Albert refused to attend, and then let Albert review them later on. Albert trusted Marcel completely, sharing his new ideas in the hope that Marcel would give him valuable feedback.

Marcel Grossmann

WHAT IS THERMODYNAMICS?

Thermodynamics is the study of temperature in relation to energy. It deals with the movement of energy from one place to another, and the change from one form to another. Heat is considered the flow of energy that can be turned into a specific amount to be used for work. "Work" is what happens in order to change something about an object.

The result of this collaboration was two new publications on Albert's original theory of relativity.

DID YOU KNOW?

Albert was made a German citizen again when he was elected to the Prussian Academy of Sciences.

Albert received an amazing opportunity in 1915—a chance for a full professorship at the University of Berlin. One of the people responsible for making this offer was Max Planck, a leading physicist of the day. Planck was also a great believer in Albert's talents. Albert had received many offers at this time, but the one from Berlin sounded too good for him to pass up. First, he would only have to teach whatever classes he chose (or none at all, if he preferred). Second, right from the start he would receive the highest possible salary for a person in his position. Third, he would become a member in the Prussian Academy of Sciences, the most respected scientific institution in Germany at the time. Perhaps best of all, though, he would be allowed as much time as he wanted to work on his theories.

When Albert was first offered the position at the University of Berlin, he wanted some time to think it over. One of the reasons he hesitated was because he disliked the German education system, which he felt was too inflexible compared to that of other European nations. He promised Planck that he would make a final decision in a few days.

MAX PLANCK

Max Planck (1858–1947) was a German physicist. His greatest contribution to the field concerned quantum theory. This dealt with the behavior of light and matter at the atomic and subatomic levels. It earned him the Nobel Prize in Physics in 1918.

The way he would reveal his decision was most unusual. When Planck and another physicist named Walther Nernst returned to Zurich, Albert would be waiting for them at the train station. If he was holding a red rose, it meant he accepted the position, but a white rose meant he decided to stay in Switzerland. Planck and Nernst were deeply relieved when they got off the train to find Albert with a red rose in hand.

On a professional level, Albert was probably more content than he had ever been. His personal life, however, was falling apart. His wife, Mileva, had not been happy with all the moves their family had made to accommodate Albert's different teaching posts. She also did not like the amount of time Albert was spending with his colleagues rather than with her and their two sons. By the time the professorship in Berlin was offered, Albert and Mileva's marriage was all but over. They moved to Berlin in April 1915 so Albert could start his new job.

By June of that year, Mileva and Albert would separate. She and the two boys moved back to Switzerland. After the breakdown of his family, Albert focused harder than ever on his work.

A new center for the study of physics called the Kaiser Wilhelm Institute for Physics was supposed to open in 1914, but the outbreak of World War I (1914–18) put these plans on hold. When the Institute finally did open in 1917, Albert was asked to be its director. He also became the president of the German Physical Society.

WORLD WAR I

World War I was a global conflict that lasted from 1914 to 1918. It involved nearly 50 countries and resulted in the death of more than 41 million people.

Plane used during the war.

In spite of all these new responsibilities, Albert still focused most of his energy on his latest theories. One of his most promising was an addition to his theory of general relativity. He had been attempting to calculate the degree to which light from a star will be bent by the gravitational force of the sun. This would become known as "gravitational lensing." Put simply, if light from a distant source is coming toward you and there is a large object between you and the light, the gravitational field from that mass will change the course of that light (often referred to as "bending" the light).

DID YOU KNOW?

Albert wrote a letter protesting World War I, but only three other scientists signed it.

There had already been a theory for centuries about this phenomenon, but Albert calculated that the effect was greater than had long been thought. He presented this idea in a book published in early 1917 called *On the Special and the General Theory of Relativity, Generally*

Comprehensible. It was written not just for the academics, but was also simplified to the point that an ordinary person with some knowledge of physics could understand it. Still, Albert's new theory would need to be proven before it could be accepted by the scientific community.

To settle the matter, a pair of English astronomers named Arthur Eddington and Frank Dyson traveled to the island of Principe, off the west coast of Africa, to observe the solar eclipse of May 29, 1919. During the eclipse—which lasted less than seven minutes—they took many photographs of the stars that were visible closest to the sun. Using the positions of

WHAT IS A SOLAR ECLIPSE?

A solar eclipse happens when the moon moves between the sun and the Earth. When this occurs, it blocks the light from the sun. A total eclipse blocks all of the light, while a partial eclipse only blocks some of it.

the stars to compare the old theory to Albert's new one, they discovered that Albert's theory that light would bend was correct. When they published these findings a few months later, the story was reported around the world—and Albert went from professor to international celebrity almost overnight.

Chapter 6

A HOUSEHOLD name

The 1920s would be a very busy time for Albert. Now that his theories of relativity had been established, he was truly famous.

Albert was now so well-known that he was bombarded with requests to travel and make appearances all over the world. Thousands of people wanted to see the great man in person and hear him speak.

Albert wasn't only a celebrity in the academic world. His reach went well beyond that. Millions of ordinary people now knew the name of Albert Einstein as well.

Albert going for a walk in 1920.

World War I had ended shortly before—in November 1918—with Germany on one side and Great Britain on the other. Many people were particularly inspired by the fact that Albert was German, and the tests to prove his calculations on the gravitational lens effect were carried out by two British men. Here were scientists from both sides of the war working together to change humankind's understanding of science and the universe! Everyone agreed that it made for a wonderful story.

Albert began his whirlwind tour of the United States in the spring of 1921. He sailed from the Netherlands in March and landed in New York City, where he was mobbed by nearly 20,000 adoring fans!

It was likely a joyous time for him, not only because of the warm American reception, but also because, in 1919, he had married again. The woman's name was Elsa Löwenthal, and she would remain faithfully at his side until her death in 1936. Albert and Elsa stayed in America for two months, starting in the northeastern area and gradually making their way to the Midwest. During this time, Albert gave lectures at some of the most respected universities in the country, including Columbia and Princeton. He was also invited to the White House to visit then-president Warren G. Harding.

When Albert visited New York City in 1921, he was welcomed by thousands of fans.

Albert during his tour of the United States, with President Warren G. Harding at the White House, Washington, D.C.

In 1921, Albert was told that he had been selected for the Nobel Prize in Physics. He was given the prize for his general contributions to theoretical physics, but specifically for his work on the "photoelectric effect." The photoelectric effect occurs when light strikes a surface (usually metal) at a certain frequency so that it causes electrons to be released from that surface. Albert wrote about this in his first "miracle year" paper in 1905.

Many of Albert's theories in relativity were still considered too controversial. So the Nobel Committee focused on Albert's work with the photoelectric effect instead.

Albert wasn't happy about this, and when he went to Sweden to accept the award, he once again showed off his rebellious side. During his acceptance speech, he talked about his relativity theories instead of the photoelectric effect, much to the shock of everyone present!

THE NOBEL PRIZE

The Nobel Prize is awarded every year, in a variety of categories, to people who have made outstanding contributions to their particular field of study. Other categories include literature, chemistry, economics, and peace. It is considered by many to be the most prestigious award in the world.

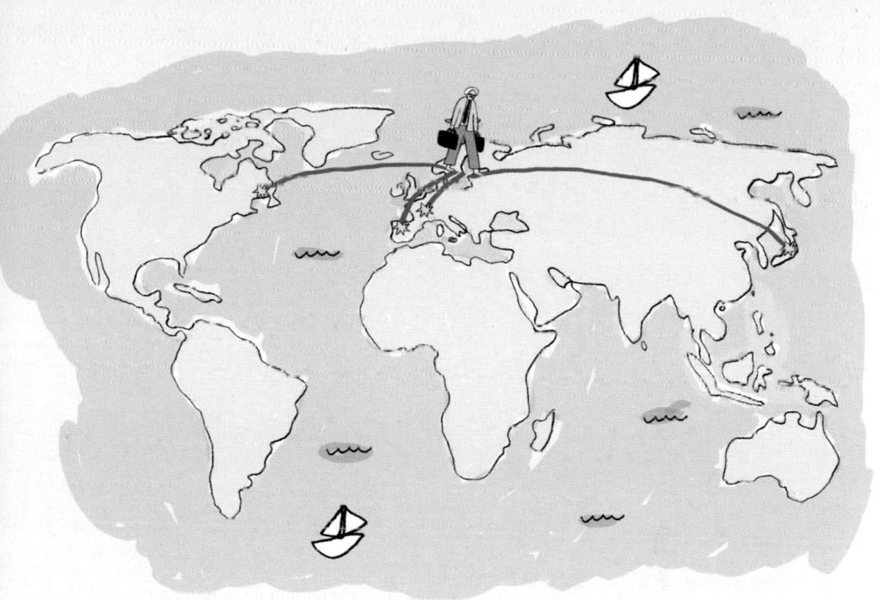

Albert continued his journey throughout the world, traveling to numerous countries including France, Spain, and Japan. He also made sure to use the attention he was suddenly getting to highlight the importance of peace and international cooperation. Years earlier, he made it clear that he was disgusted by the horrors of World War I. He was also angry at his academic colleagues who supported it. In 1915, he wrote a paper unrelated to physics titled, "My Opinion of the War." In it, he argued that a tendency toward violence in males was the cause of warfare.

Now that he had thousands of people listening to his every word, he often spoke about the importance of finding a way for all nations to exist peacefully together. He also joined a group called the "Committee on Intellectual Cooperation." It was a part of the League of Nations, an organization formed at the end of World War I. The Committee's purpose was to discuss ideas on how world peace might be achieved.

Albert used his connections through the League of Nations to encourage scientists of all fields to work across national borders for the sake of exchanging ideas, to move science forward without interference from politics.

LEAGUE OF NATIONS

The League of Nations was an organization created in 1920, in the aftermath of World War I. Its purpose was to encourage peace and cooperation between the countries of the world. Although it only lasted until 1946, it inspired the founding of the United Nations.

Meeting of the League of Nations in Geneva, 1926. The League of Nations was founded on January 10, 1920.

Another benefit to scientists working together would be the introduction of people to different cultures. As a result, people would learn to become more understanding of cultural differences, and less likely to use them as an excuse for war.

Albert spent some time in the 1920s focusing on cosmology. In simple terms, this is the study of the beginnings and continuing progression of the universe. While the notion of cosmology had been around for centuries, Albert modernized it starting in 1917 with his paper "Cosmological Considerations of the General Theory of Relativity." Not many people paid attention to it at first, mostly because it wasn't easy to find outside of Germany until World War I ended. However, more scientists took notice of it after Albert won the Nobel Prize and reached the status of an international celebrity.

One of the most important points Albert made in the paper was that he believed the universe was not of any fixed, permanent size, but rather that it was continually expanding. Again, he was challenging a very old and long-accepted idea—and again, the academic community decided his theory needed to be proven before it could be accepted.

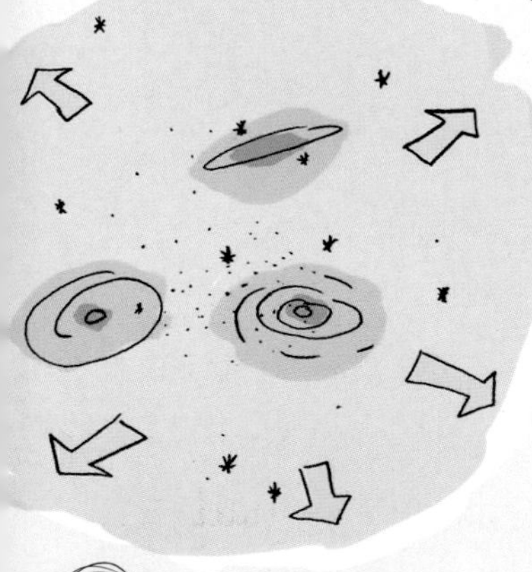

This was accomplished in 1929 by respected astronomer Edwin Hubble. A dedicated worker, Hubble used a newly built telescope at the Mount Wilson Observatory in

Astronomer Edwin Hubble looks into the telescope at the Mount Wilson Observatory, 1937.

Washington State to study a variety of astronomical bodies, such as stars and galaxies. After noticing shifts in their position and distance, he realized he had found evidence that the universe was, in fact, growing in size. Once again, Albert was right!

While Albert's reputation around the world continued to grow, so did his passion for religious and philosophical thought. Where religion was concerned, he considered himself a believer of some sort of supreme intelligence. However, he didn't trust organized religion because he feared that it would be too easy to use it to manipulate people for evil purposes. He was still Jewish, but he was interested in other faiths as well. He felt that one religion alone was not the path to a person's spiritual contentment. He was also fascinated with all sorts of philosophical ideas, on everything from what it means to be human to understanding the difference between right and wrong.

All of this came from his tireless curiosity about the secrets of life, humanity, and the universe. His celebrity status gave him access to all different sorts of people from every corner of the world. While his kind of open-minded thinking was appreciated by many people, it was viewed as downright dangerous by others—including some who awaited Albert's return back in Germany.

Writer, musician, and painter Rabindranath Tagore visiting Albert in Caputh, 1930.

Albert with English actor Charlie Chaplin in 1931.

Albert with his second wife Elsa (left) and famous psychic Gene Dennis (right) in 1932.

Chapter 7

A man without a country

Albert was against the idea of war in any form. Because of this, he was about to enter one of the most difficult times of his life.

As the 1920s became the 1930s, many Germans were very unhappy. Germany had come out on the losing side of World War I, and as a result they had been forced to agree to some very harsh terms.

One condition was that they had to pay for much of the damage that they had caused during the war. Another was that they were not allowed to have military power anymore. They had to give back a lot of the land they had acquired in previous years from other countries. They also had to publicly admit that they were responsible for the war. Most of these conditions were outlined in a document called the Treaty of Versailles. The effects of the Treaty of Versailles led Germany into terrible times.

Their economy collapsed, leaving many citizens so poor that they could barely afford to eat. Millions lost their jobs, crime was on the rise, and the general mood of the nation became gloomy and hopeless. Most Germans began to feel anger toward those they felt were responsible for their misery.

Crowds of concerned Germans waiting outside a bank in Berlin, 1931.

TREATY OF VERSAILLES

The signing of the Treaty of Versailles on June 28, 1919, marked the end of World War I. Since the Germans lost the war, the conditions of the Treaty were decided by the side that won—the Allies. The agreement set down very harsh terms for the German nation. It required Germany to pay for much of the damage caused by the war, which left the German people in an economic depression that lasted for years.

One person who took advantage of this anger was a man named Adolf Hitler. At one time a homeless artist selling his work on the streets of Vienna, Hitler had since become a politician. After the Germans surrendered in World War I, and then signed the Treaty of Versailles, Hitler became enraged at those who, he claimed, "stabbed Germany in the back." He began to form a list of those he felt were

Adolf Hitler

responsible—he targeted Jews, intellectuals, Romany people, and others.

Hitler joined the National Socialist German Workers' Party, which would eventually become known as the Nazi Party. He was a strong public speaker, and he quickly rose through Nazi ranks to become their leader. He used his speaking skills to encourage the anger of the German people, and he soon became the leader of the entire country.

DID YOU KNOW?

When Hitler joined the Nazi Party in 1920, there were fewer than 60 members, but by 1945, there were more than 8.5 million.

After imprisoning or murdering all of his political opponents, he held total power. Then he began to put in place new policies. These were designed to persecute, or target, any people who, in Hitler's opinion, made the country weaker—including Jews and intellectuals.

Germany became a dangerous place to live for many people, including Albert. He was both a Jew and an intellectual, so he was exactly the sort of person the Nazi Party was persecuting.

Although Albert was a German citizen, he spent less and less time there. He was deeply worried by the anti-Semitism, or hatred of Jews, that was being stirred up by Hitler. He had built a house in the quiet German village of Caputh in 1929, but between his travels and his work at other universities, he wasn't there much. By 1931, two of his positions meant he had to be either in Pasadena, California or Oxford, England.

In 1932, Albert met a man named Abraham Flexner, who informed him about a new

Albert's summer house in the German village of Caputh, 2005.

educational research center being set up in Princeton, New Jersey. It was called the Institute for Advanced Study, or "IAS" for short, and it would be dedicated to international scientific research. Albert was asked to be part of this exciting new program, and he was considering the position.

Institute for Advanced Study

He had planned to divide his time between Germany and Princeton. However, everything changed in early 1933, when Hitler began forcing Jews out of academic posts and forbidding them from holding other important positions. Then the Nazis froze Albert's bank account and seized his property in Caputh. For Albert, that was the last straw. He resigned his membership from the Prussian Academy of Sciences—even though it was one of the most prestigious academies in the world. The Nazis

Albert's life was in danger even during his time in England. He was guarded by men with guns.

began showing their hatred of him by publicly burning the books he had written. Fearing for his safety, Albert fled to Belgium, where he gave up his German citizenship for the second time. He then went to England, where friends protected him night and day. At one point, he was guarded by men with shotguns!

During this time, Albert was concerned for more than just his own safety. He was also deeply worried about other scientists who had so far been unable to leave Hitler's Germany. Not long after renouncing his own German citizenship, he met with Winston Churchill, who was British prime minister at the time. Albert asked him for help, so Churchill sent a trusted friend to Germany to bring as many Jewish scientists back to England as possible. Then Albert wrote letters to the leaders of other nations asking for the same assistance.

However, Albert did not stay in England for very long. He soon realized he was still putting himself in danger by remaining in the country.

ALBERT THE REFUGEE

Many people don't realize that Albert was a refugee—a very famous one! Even after he settled in the United States, his concern for other refugees never stopped. He and his wife, Elsa, filled out many visa applications for Jews trying to escape Germany. He also used his celebrity status to help others whenever he could.

DID YOU KNOW?

Hitler put a bounty, or reward, on Albert's life, offering the equivalent of $5,000 to anyone who found and killed him.

There were rumors that Hitler not only wished to drive all Jews out of Germany, but also force them out of Europe altogether. There was also a suspicion that Hitler hoped to one day take over the entire continent.

All these horrible possibilities played a big role in Albert finally deciding to accept Abraham Flexner's offer to come to work in Princeton. The Institute for Advanced Study was up and running when Albert finally arrived in October 1933. It is likely he felt particularly safe there, since they had already hired many other Jewish scientists who were fleeing Nazi persecution.

Over the next few years, Albert was offered other positions at different universities around the world. He declined them all, however, and decided to stay in Princeton for good in 1935. Then in 1936, he requested—and would eventually receive—full citizenship in the United States.

Albert lived in this house in Princeton, New Jersey, from 1935 until his death in 1955.

Albert the American

Albert settled into American life very quickly. He particularly liked the general attitudes and many freedoms of the United States.

Albert was impressed with the privilege of being able to speak your mind openly and without fear. Back in Germany, the Nazi Party was planting spies throughout the towns and cities to assure that no one publicly criticized Hitler or his policies. Those who did so could expect quick and severe punishment.

In the United States, Albert felt that people were encouraged to express themselves and open their minds to new ideas. He also liked the way average people could get ahead if they worked hard and developed their professional skills.

In other places where he had been, he found it ridiculous that people could make more money or get into positions of power simply because of the people they knew.

Once he was settled in the United States and away from the threat of Nazism, Albert could once again focus on developing his latest theories. One, which he had begun tinkering with in the late 1920s, was known as a "unified field theory," or UFT. If he was successful, his UFT would be able to basically predict natural phenomena, such as the movement of objects in the universe. It came from a desire to take all the different theories of physics and essentially combine them into one great equation.

THE THEORY OF EVERYTHING

The "unified field theory," in very simple terms, was Albert's attempt to explain the way all the forces of the universe acted upon all physical things. He worked on it for many years, and it became known as his "Theory of Everything."

Albert at his first lecture for the Institute for Advanced Study, 1933.

Another of Albert's academic highlights was the 1935 publication of the "Einstein-Podolsky-Rosen Paradox" (or EPR Paradox for short), on which Albert worked with two other physicists—Boris Podolsky and Nathan Rosen. Together, the three of them used the EPR Paradox to question quantum mechanics (QM).

---

what is quantum mechanics?

In basic terms, quantum mechanics (QM) explains how atoms, and things made up of atoms, work. QM also attempts to explain how electromagnetic waves, such as light, function.

Albert and his wife, Elsa, in 1932.

While Albert enjoyed living in America, not all of his time proved to be happy. His marriage to Elsa had provided him with the emotional support he needed to do his work for many years. Not long after he and Elsa moved into their new home on Mercer Street in Princeton, she began to feel seriously ill. Several doctor visits and tests later, it was determined that Elsa had developed both heart and kidney disease. Albert tried to be as helpful as he could, but the emotional strain of seeing his beloved wife suffering led him to focus more closely on his work than ever. Elsa passed away on December 20, 1936, leaving Albert broken-hearted. A close friend of the couple said he saw Albert crying in the aftermath of the loss, something he had never known Albert to do before.

DID YOU KNOW?

The FBI was worried about Albert's political beliefs. They even kept a secret file on him!

In spite of Albert's love for America and its many freedoms, there was one aspect of the country that he felt needed to change—racism. Racism is the hatred of a group of people based solely on their skin color or ethnicity. America's past was full of horrific racist incidents, which included everything from refusing people service at a restaurant to burning down their homes, beating them, or even killing them.

As someone who believed in civil rights and that all people had equal value, Albert found this completely unacceptable. He remembered all too well the racism directed at Jews in Hitler's Germany, and he was afraid that he was seeing people behave in a similar way in his new country.

What are civil rights?

Equality and freedom for all people. Many people in the US at this time did not have the same basic civil rights that white people did.

Albert began his anti-racist mission right in his own town of Princeton. It didn't take long for him to realize that Princeton, at that time, was highly segregated. Segregation is the practice of keeping different races separate from each other, even if they live together in the same community.

Princeton had its "black neighborhood," separate from where white families lived. Some businesses would only serve white customers. For example, black people often had to buy their groceries in different stores.

Marian Anderson

Albert found all of this appalling, and he was very outspoken about his views on segregation. He believed that it was a "disease" caused by the attitudes of white people, and he would later say, "I do not intend to be quiet about it."

Albert treated everyone with equal consideration and stood up for those who were treated unfairly. When singer Marian Anderson came to Princeton and was refused a hotel room because of her race, Albert invited her to stay in his home. He even paid the tuition of a young black student who could not afford to attend university. In addition, he joined the National Association for the Advancement of Colored People (NAACP).

Albert would continue to fight against racism in America in the years ahead. In the late 1930s, however, he was very worried about what was happening on the other side

WHAT IS THE NAACP?

The National Association for the Advancement of Colored People (NAACP) is an American organization whose mission is to protect people from race-based discrimination. It was founded in 1909, and is America's oldest civil rights organization.

of the world. In Germany, Hitler, the man responsible for driving Albert and millions of other Jews out of the country, was becoming more powerful than ever.

Using violence and racism, Hitler was working hard to take over Europe. His terrifying goal was to remove Jewish people and anyone else that he did not consider worthy. In spite of this twisted thinking, Hitler and his Nazi followers were making remarkable progress—and Albert knew it had to be stopped before it was too late.

Chapter 9

The Manhattan Project

Albert had spent his whole life believing that armed conflict of any kind was wrong, but his beliefs were about to be tested.

Albert was a strong believer in pacifism, which means that he was against war and thought that people should find peaceful ways to work out their differences. Following the rise of Hitler, however, his beliefs were challenged. In Germany, Hitler and the Nazis were targeting and attacking Jews in many different ways. They destroyed Jewish synagogues and businesses, and they arrested and murdered people of the Jewish faith.

By the end of the 1930s, Hitler's Nazis had taken over many of Germany's neighboring countries. This lead to the start of World War II (1939–45).

Deeply worried about the horrific events unfolding in Europe, Albert and another German-Jewish physicist, Leo Szilard, sent a letter to then-US president Franklin D. Roosevelt. In the letter, they warned Roosevelt that Hitler was working with scientists who supported Nazism to develop an atomic bomb. This was now possible because of the recent discovery of nuclear fission—a process during which an atom releases huge amounts of energy after being split.

Leo Szilard

A mushroom cloud rising after an atomic bomb test.

DID YOU KNOW?

Like Albert, physicist Leo Szilard was a refugee who had fled from Nazi Germany.

Physicists quickly realized the destructive power of nuclear fission, and Szilard conducted a series of experiments at Columbia University in New York to prove this. He figured out that uranium—an easily mined mineral within the Earth—would be ideal for an atomic bomb. Its atoms could be split to produce a great amount of power. As a result, an explosion of massive size and force could be created. If the Nazi scientists could create such a weapon, Hitler would have the power to take over every country in the world.

Roosevelt immediately understood the danger of the situation and created the Advisory Committee on Uranium. This was the start of what would eventually become known as the Manhattan Project. The Manhattan Project was the American-led project to develop an atomic weapon. It was run by the Army Corps of Engineers as of June 1942.

The Manhattan Project grew into one of the most important military developments in history. It was supported not only by the US government, but also by Great Britain and Canada. With only a few dozen workers at the beginning, it had more than 125,000 at the end. It also used the talents of some of the most respected scientists of the day, including Enrico Fermi, Richard Feynman, and J. Robert Oppenheimer. Albert, however, was not part of it. Because he was a pacifist, the government did not want to give him information about it. In fact, the project was conducted in such secrecy that Albert never even knew about it—until August 1945, that is.

Dr. J. Robert Oppenheimer and General Leslie Groves (right) inspecting an atomic bomb site, 1945.

By 1945, the Nazis were losing the war. Finally, in April, soldiers from the Soviet Union surrounded the German capital of Berlin. Hitler chose to take his own life rather than be captured, and Germany surrendered shortly after that.

Japan, however, was determined to continue the war in the Pacific. US president Harry S. Truman (Roosevelt had died by this point) realized that this could mean many more years of fighting. So, he decided to allow the military to use two of the atomic bombs created through the Manhattan Project.

Hot off the press—Allied soldiers read about Germany's surrender in *The Stars and Stripes* military newspaper, May 1945.

This aircraft dropped the atomic bomb on Hiroshima.

The bombs were dropped on August 6, 1945, on the Japanese city of Hiroshima, and on August 9, 1945, on Japan's seaport town of Nagasaki. The use of the bombs forced Japan to surrender, officially ending World War II. However, the death toll—thought to be as high as a quarter of a million Japanese citizens—filled Albert with tremendous regret. Although it was Szilard who wrote the letter to Roosevelt that led to the development of the bombs, Albert knew it was the strength of his own support that helped get the president's attention. When Albert realized that his research was used to help create the most destructive weapon in history, his regret only deepened. In his later years, he would consider his support of the

DID YOU KNOW?

Albert did not even know about the Manhattan Project until August of 1945, when the bombs were dropped.

bombs' development the greatest mistake of his life—yet he still felt it had to be done in order to stop Hitler from developing one first.

It didn't take Albert long to realize that the world was entering a new age following the development of the atomic bomb. What this meant was that humans were now capable of immense power that could destroy the world around them. Because of this, people would need to use that power responsibly.

To encourage this, Albert got involved with the National Committee on Atomic Information, which represented dozens of educational, civic, and religious organizations. Since the development of the atomic bomb had been a secret project from the beginning, ordinary citizens did not know of its existence until bombs were used to end the war. Because of the terrifying power of atomic energy, Albert felt it was essential to educate the public.

Albert and seven other leading scientists pictured at a lunch given by the Emergency Committee of Atomic Scientists.

He and other like-minded scientists (including Leo Szilard) also formed a group known as the Emergency Committee of Atomic Scientists in May 1946. This second organization would continue to educate the public and further encourage world leaders to work together peacefully, rather than make use of more atomic bombs in the future. In the years ahead, Albert would use his name to

request funding that would help the committees with their goals. He also asked the United Nations (UN) to set rules that would help limit the atomic capabilities of any country that would eventually have the bomb. The UN's failure to do this, however, along with too little funding, forced the committee to break up in 1951.

Albert, however, would continue to publicly state his firm belief that peace was the only true pathway to assuring humanity's survival.

"Mankind must **give up war** in the Atomic Era. What is at stake is the **life or death of humanity.**"

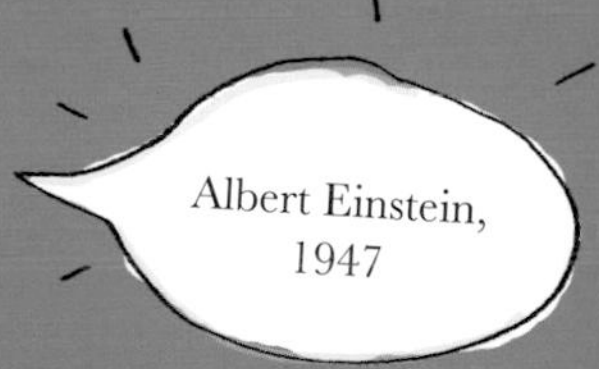

Albert Einstein, 1947

Chapter 10

Final years

While most people tend to slow down in their later years, Albert stayed busy. His curiosity and enthusiasm never disappeared.

Albert spent the last years of his life doing the things he loved the most—working on his theories, publicly supporting his most passionate political causes, and enjoying his favorite hobbies.

Albert adored music—Mozart and Bach were his favorite composers. He also enjoyed playing his violin, and would continue to do so into old age. He wasn't the greatest player, but he was

Albert playing the violin.

truly passionate about it. Music also helped him to think more clearly when working out his theories.

One of the ideas that he continued to develop was his unified field theory (UFT). He wanted it not only to tie together all the major laws of physics in one neat concept, but also to alter the very basis of quantum mechanics. Albert would never complete his work on his famous "Theory of Everything," and it remains unresolved.

Albert also continued his support of Jews worldwide. He helped to raise money for Jewish causes, such as the establishment of a Jewish homeland. The number of Jewish deaths caused by Nazi persecution could not be calculated at the time, but today it is estimated to be somewhere in the neighborhood of six million. After World War II, many Jewish people who were fortunate enough to escape Nazi influence had scattered to various parts of the globe.

Because of the horrors they had to endure during World War II, Jewish people felt the need for a homeland of their own.

This would become a reality in 1948, when the United States, under the leadership of then-US president Harry S. Truman, recognized the nation of Israel as the official Jewish state. Israel is located on ancient land neighbored by Lebanon, Syria, Jordan, Egypt, and Palestine, as well as the Mediterranean Sea.

Israel's first president was a man named Chaim Weizmann, who started his career as a chemist before turning to politics. When Weizmann died in 1952, Israel's prime minister, David Ben-Gurion, asked Albert to be Weizmann's replacement. Israel's government had a parliamentary structure, which meant that

1968 bank note from Israel with Albert's face on it.

Prime Minister of Israel David Ben-Gurion visits Albert in Princeton in 1951. He would later offer Albert the position of President of Israel.

the prime minister had most of the "real" power, while the president's post was mainly for show. The thinking was that Albert's fame, as well as his accomplishments, would be good publicity for Israel in the years to come. Albert was also promised that he would still be able to continue his work in physics.

The main problem with the offer, however, was that he would have to give up his life in Princeton and move to Israel, where he would have to become an Israeli citizen. While Albert was touched by the offer, he had little choice but to politely reject it. Albert was aware that his mind was geared more toward science than politics, so he chose to stay in Princeton.

Back home in Princeton, one of the hobbies he enjoyed was sailing. The funny thing was, he didn't have much talent for it. He owned a small sailboat, which he would take out into quiet waters and just sort of drift around. Those who knew about this said he did it mostly so he could become isolated, giving him an opportunity to

think and jot down his latest ideas. Since he had no real sailing skill, though, he often got himself into trouble. He would get lost, run aground, or slam into other people's boats because he wasn't paying attention.

As active as Albert was, however, he was beginning to experience some health issues, and he knew his time was becoming very limited. Albert had had surgery in 1948 to treat an aneurysm—the weakening of an artery, through which blood flows—in his abdomen. On April 15, 1955, however, the reinforcement of that aneurysm finally gave out, causing it to rupture, or break. This led to a bout of severe internal bleeding.

Although Albert was rushed to Princeton Hospital, he refused to have the surgery required to treat it. At the time, he said, "It is tasteless to prolong life artificially. I have done my share, it is time to go." He eventually lost consciousness and passed away on the morning of April 18, 1955, at the age of 76.

Albert Einstein is considered by many to be the greatest mind of the 20th century. He changed the way we look at the universe, and his theories are the basis of modern physics. His unique thoughts on matter, energy, space, time, and gravity also proved to the world that those who think differently are often the ones who make the biggest difference.

Albert is also remembered as a kindhearted soul who cared deeply for humanity. He had a tireless desire to see people of all races live together peacefully. Albert was never afraid to speak his mind, even if that meant irritating other people. Perhaps that was his true genius—if he had an idea that he believed was correct, he would follow it through. Whatever words we use to describe him, one thing's for sure—he made the world a better place in the time that he was here.

Albert's family tree

Mileva Marić
1875–1948

First wife

Daughter

Lieserl Einstein
1902–?

Hans Albert Einstein
1904–1973

Son

Son

Eduard Einstein
1910–1965

Father

Hermann Einstein
1847–1902

Mother

Pauline Koch
1858–1920

Albert Einstein

1879–1955

Albert was his parents' first child and only son.

Sister

Maria "Maja" Einstein
1881–1951

Second wife

Elsa Löwenthal
1876–1936

Step-daughter

Ilse Löwenthal
1897–1934

Step-daughter

Margot Löwenthal
1900–1986

Timeline

1879
Albert Einstein is born in a small town called Ulm, Germany, on March 14.

1881
Albert's younger sister, Maria (Maja), is born.

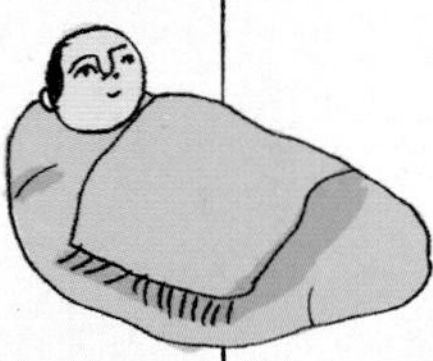

1888
Albert begins his studies at the Luitpold Gymnasium (Munich) at the age of 9.

1896
Albert enrolls in the Swiss Federal Polytechnic School.

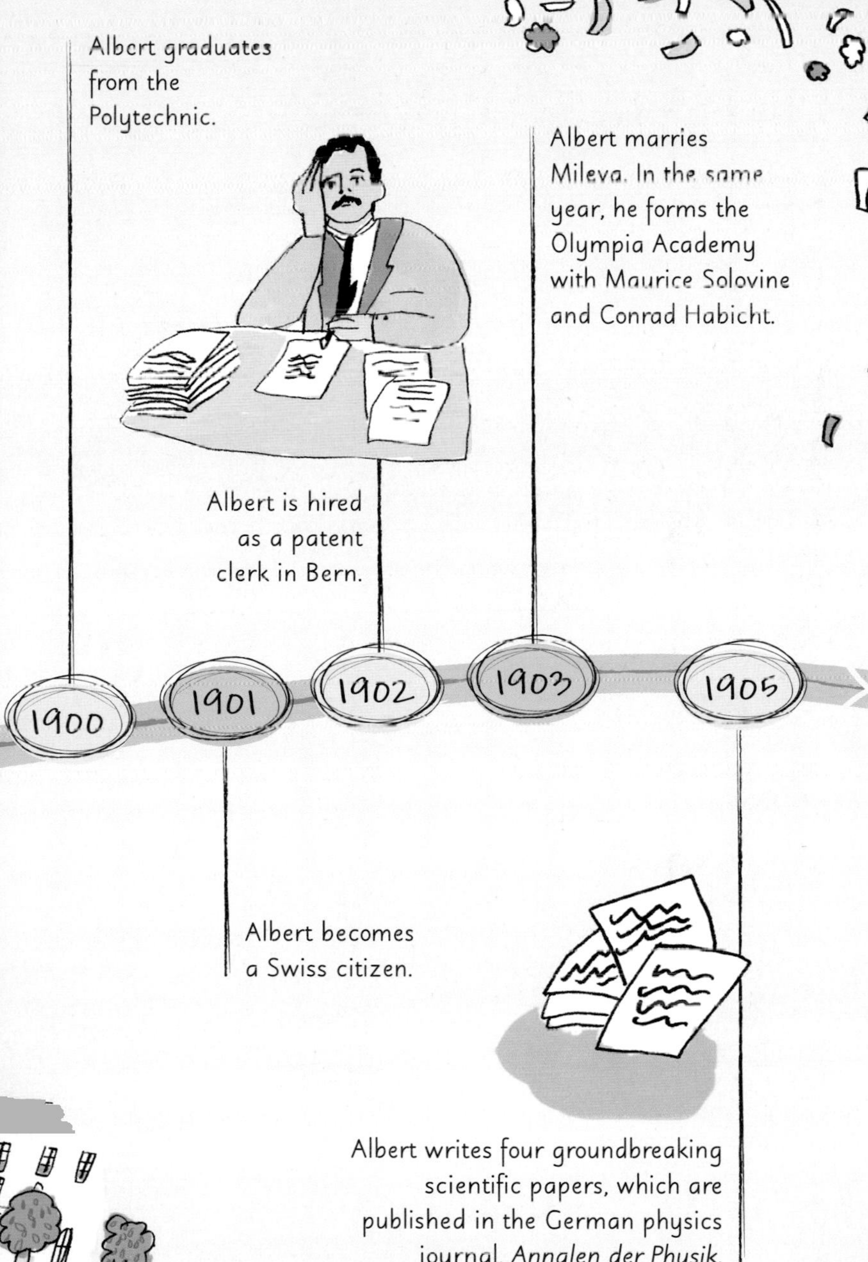

1900

Albert graduates from the Polytechnic.

1901

Albert becomes a Swiss citizen.

1902

Albert is hired as a patent clerk in Bern.

1903

Albert marries Mileva. In the same year, he forms the Olympia Academy with Maurice Solovine and Conrad Habicht.

1905

Albert writes four groundbreaking scientific papers, which are published in the German physics journal, *Annalen der Physik*.

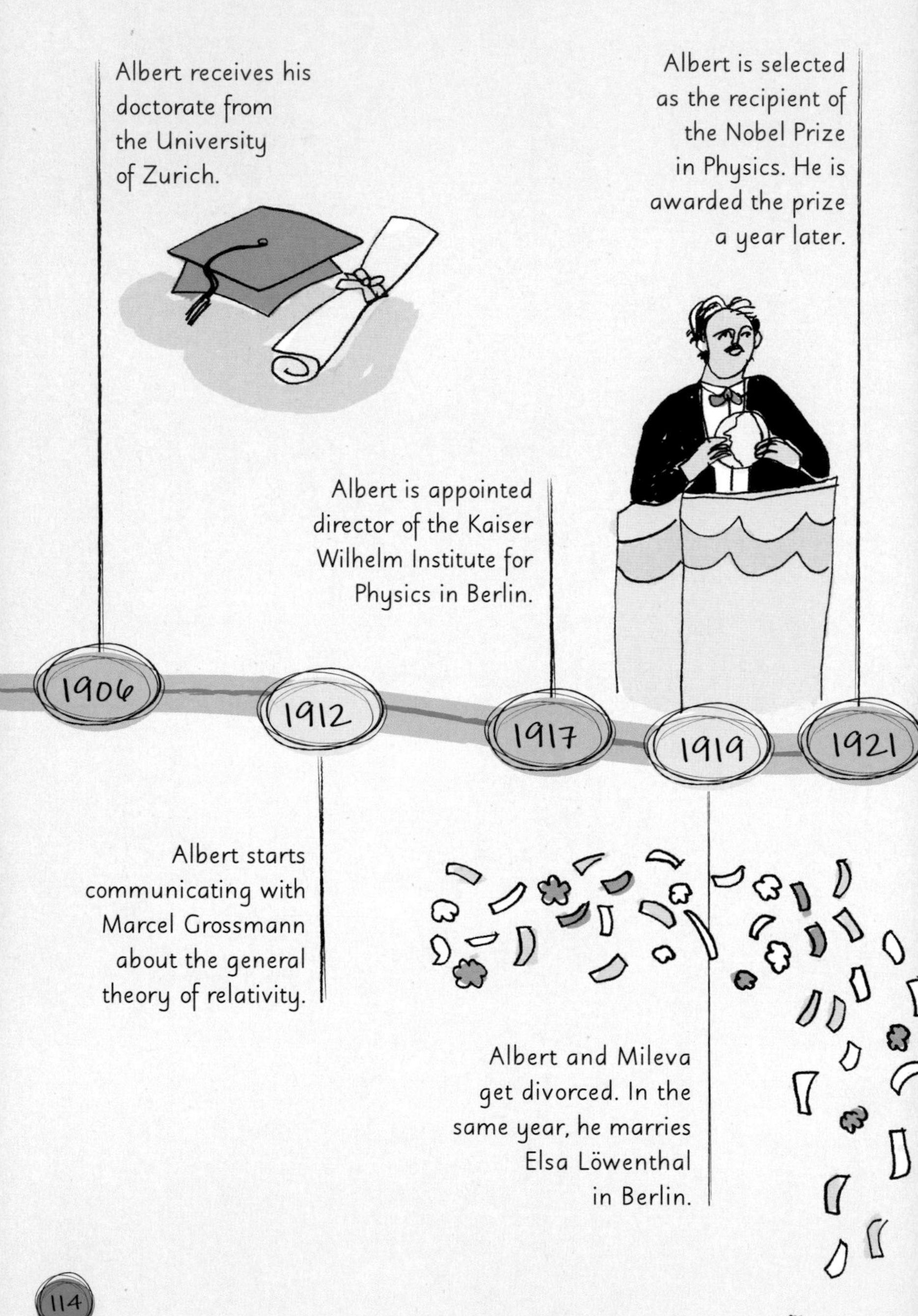
1906
Albert receives his doctorate from the University of Zurich.
1912
Albert starts communicating with Marcel Grossmann about the general theory of relativity.
1917
Albert is appointed director of the Kaiser Wilhelm Institute for Physics in Berlin.
1919
Albert and Mileva get divorced. In the same year, he marries Elsa Löwenthal in Berlin.
1921
Albert is selected as the recipient of the Nobel Prize in Physics. He is awarded the prize a year later.

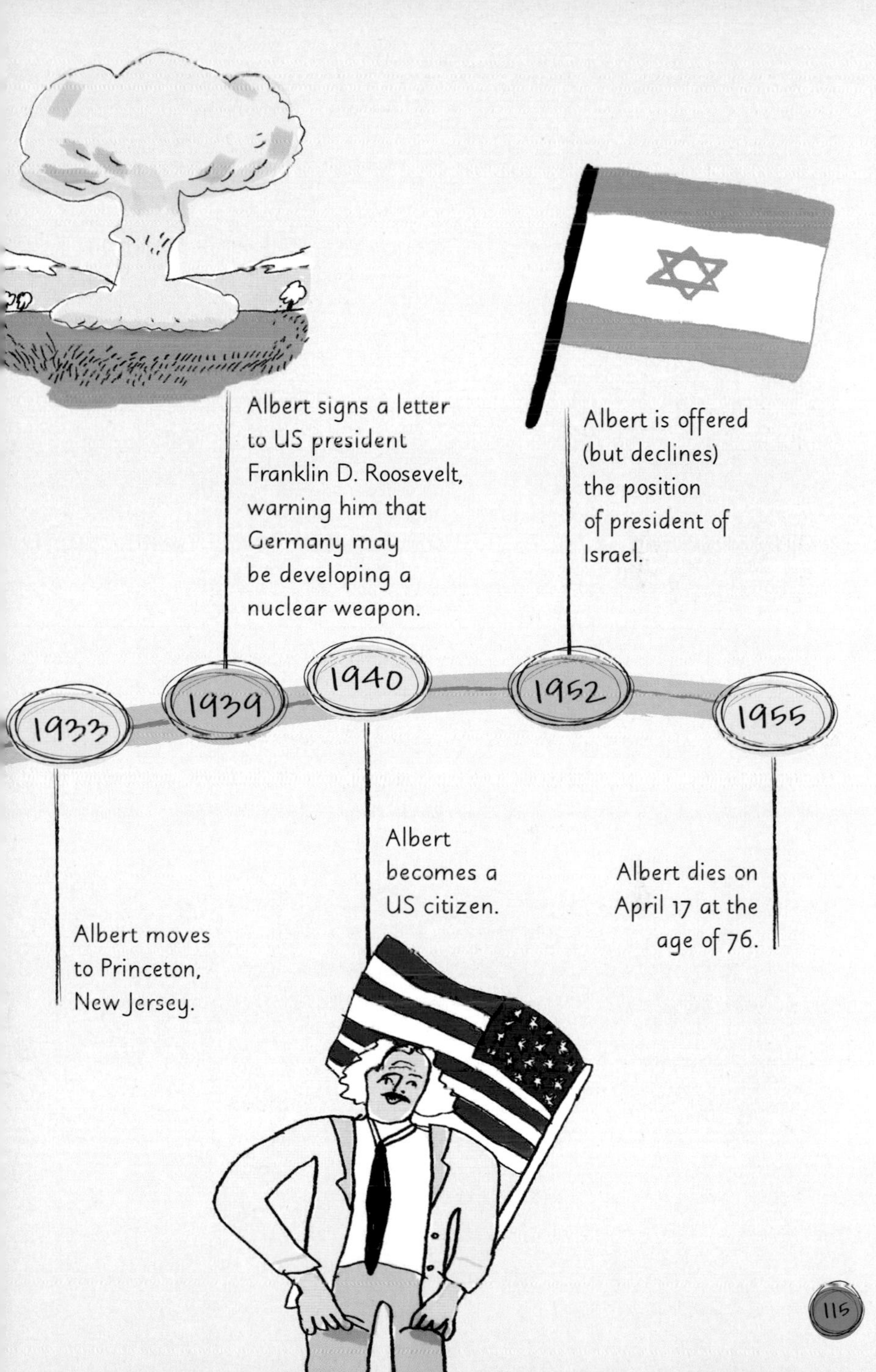
Albert signs a letter to US president Franklin D. Roosevelt, warning him that Germany may be developing a nuclear weapon.
Albert is offered (but declines) the position of president of Israel.
1933
1939
1940
1952
1955
Albert moves to Princeton, New Jersey.
Albert becomes a US citizen.
Albert dies on April 17 at the age of 76.

1. What were the names of Albert's parents?

2. What nickname did the Einsteins' maid give Albert when he was little?

3. What was the name of the first school Albert attended?

4. Who taught Albert to play the violin, and encouraged his love of music?

5. Name the group that Albert formed with Maurice Solovine and Conrad Habicht.

6. How many groundbreaking papers did Albert publish during his "miracle year"?

7. For which equation is Albert most famous?

Do you remember what you've read? How many of these questions about Albert's life can you answer?

8. What type of flower did Albert use to show that he accepted the position at the University of Berlin?

9. In which country was Albert protected by men with guns?

10. In which US town did Albert live?

11. What was the name of the US-led project to develop an atomic weapon?

12. Who were Albert's favorite composers?

Answers on page 128

Who's who?

Ben-Gurion, David
(1886–1973) first prime minister of Israel

Besso, Michele Angelo
(1873–1955) Swiss-Italian engineer and Albert's friend

Churchill, Winston
(1874–1965) prime minister of the UK during World War II

Dyson, Frank
(1868–1939) one of the British astronomers who proved Albert's theory of general relativity

Eddington, Arthur
(1882–1944) one of the British astronomers who proved Albert's theory of general relativity

Einstein, Eduard
(1910–1965) Albert's younger son

Einstein, Hans Albert
(1904–1973) Albert's older son

Einstein, Hermann
(1847–1902) Albert's father

Einstein, Lieserl
(1902–?) Albert's first child

Einstein, Maria "Maja"
(1881–1951) Albert's younger sister

Fermi, Enrico
(1901–1954) Italian-American physicist who worked on the Manhattan Project

Feynman, Richard
(1918–1988) American physicist who worked on the Manhattan Project

Flexner, Abraham
(1866–1959) founder of the Institute for Advanced Study

Grossmann, Marcel
(1878–1936) mathematician and Albert's classmate

Habicht, Conrad
(1876–1958) mathematician and member of the Olympia Academy

Hitler, Adolf
(1889–1945) German chancellor from 1933 to 1945 and Nazi Party leader from 1934 to 1945

Koch, Pauline
(1858–1920) Albert's mother

Laub, Jakob Johann
(1884–1962) physicist who worked with Albert on his theories of special relativity

Löwenthal, Elsa
(1876–1936) Albert's second wife

Löwenthal, Ilse
(1897–1934) Albert's older stepdaughter

Löwenthal, Margot
(1900–1986) Albert's younger stepdaughter

Marić, Mileva
(1875–1948) Albert's first wife

Oppenheimer, J. Robert
(1904–1967) American physicist and scientific director of the Manhattan Project

Planck, Max
(1858–1947) German physicist who won the 1918 Nobel Prize in Physics

Roosevelt, Franklin D.
(1882–1945) President of the United States from 1933 to 1945

Solovine, Maurice
(1875–1958) philosopher, mathematician, and member of the Olympia Academy

Szilard, Leo
(1898–1964) Hungarian-American physicist who wrote the letter encouraging the US president to develop an atomic weapon

Truman, Harry S.
(1884–1972) President of the United States from 1945 to 1953

Glossary

academic
relating to education

aneurysm
weakening of an artery

anti-Semitism
hatred of Jewish people

atom
smallest part of any element that still has all the main qualities of that element

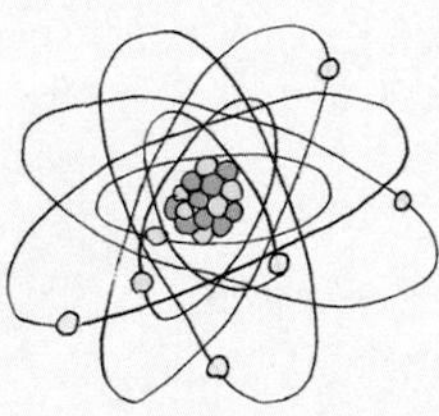

atomic bomb
powerful bomb that releases nuclear energy when it explodes

bankruptcy
when people or organizations lose all their money

calculus
method of calculating complex mathematical problems

civil rights
rights to freedom and equality given by the US Constitution

cosmology
philosophy that addresses the origins of the universe

doctorate
highest academic degree

energy
stored ability to do work

faculty
refers mostly to the teachers, and sometimes administrators, of a particular school

FBI
Federal Bureau of Investigation—part of the US government that investigates crime

gravitational lensing
the way the path of light is altered by the gravitational force of a physical body

gravity
force that causes physical objects to fall toward the Earth

Israel
Middle Eastern country set up in 1948 as a Jewish state

Manhattan Project
American-led project to develop an atomic weapon

molecule
smallest physical unit of a material

Mount Olympus
highest mountain in Greece, where the ancient Greeks believed the gods lived

Nazi
member of the National Socialist German Workers' Party, which ruled Germany under the direction of Adolf Hitler

Nobel Prize
prize given each year to a person or group who makes an outstanding contribution to their field

nuclear fission
process during which an atom releases huge amounts of energy when being split

pacifism
to be against war

particle
very tiny portion of a larger physical body

patent
legally recognized ownership of copyright for an invention or idea

PhD
abbreviation that stands for "Doctor of Philosophy," which is an academic degree

physics
study of matter and its relation to force, motion, and energy

pi
approximately 3.14—it is the circumference of any circle divided by its diameter

racism
belief that certain people are better than others because of their race, or hating a group of people because of their race

relativity
Albert's theory that motion is relative to the space around it, keeping in mind that time and space are also relative to each other

segregation
keeping people of different races or religions separate from each other

stateless
to be without citizenship of any country

thermodynamics
relationship between heat and work energy

unified field theory (UFT)
theory to tie all physics laws together in one ultimate equation; also known as the "Theory of Everything"

wave
what happens when energy moves from one place to another

Index

Aa

Aarau, Switzerland 24
Anderson, Marian 90
Annalen der Physik 35, 39, 40–41, 42–43
atomic bombs 47, 93–101
atoms 35, 44, 47

Bb

bankruptcy 22
Ben-Gurion, David 104–105
Berlin 55–57
Bern 31, 34, 40, 48, 51–52
Besso, Michele Angelo 41–42
bombs, atomic 47, 93–101

Cc

Chaplin, Charlie 73
Charles-Ferdinand University, Prague 53
Churchill, Winston 81
civil rights 88–91
compasses 10–12
cosmology 69–71

Dd

Dyson, Frank 60–61

Ee

$E=mc^2$ 45, 47
eclipses, solar 60–61
Eddington, Arthur 60–61
Einstein, Eduard (son) 37
Einstein, Hans Albert (son) 37, 40
Einstein, Hermann (father) 8–9, 22–23
Einstein, Jakob (uncle) 8
Einstein, Lieserl (daughter) 37
Einstein, Maria "Maja" (sister) 17
Einstein, Mileva (first wife) 36–39, 40, 57–58
Einstein, Pauline (mother) 8–9, 27
Einstein-Podolsky-Rosen Paradox 86
energy 39, 45, 47, 54, 93

Ff

faculty 51
Fermi, Enrico 95
Feynman, Richard 95
Flexner, Albert 78–79, 82

Gg

German Physical Society 58
gravitational lensing 59–61, 63
gravity 12, 13, 54
Grossmann, Marcel 54–55
gymnasium 20

Hh

Habicht, Conrad 33–34
Harding, Warren G. 64–65
Hiroshima 97
Hitler, Adolf 76–82, 84, 88, 91–94, 96, 98
Hubble, Edwin 70–71

Ii

Institute for Advanced Study (IAS) 79, 82–83, 86
inventions 31
Israel 104–106

Jj

Japan 30, 45, 67
Jews 15, 19, 72, 77–79, 81–82, 88, 91, 92, 103–104

Kk

Kaiser Wilhelm Institute for Physics 58

Ll

Laub, Jakob Johann 46–49
League of Nations 68–69
light 43–44, 47, 59–61, 65
Löwenthal, Elsa (second wife) 64, 73, 81, 87
Luitpold Gymnasium, Munich 20, 22–23, 25

Mm

magnetism 11–12
Manhattan Project 94–98
mass 47
molecules 35
Mount Olympus 32
Munich 15–16, 18–20, 23, 25
music 27, 102–103

Nn

Nagasaki 97
National Association for the Advancement of Colored People (NAACP) 90–91
Nazi Party 77, 79–80, 82, 84–85, 92–94, 96, 103
Nernst, Walther 57
Nobel Prize 65–66, 70
nuclear fission 93–101

Oo

Olympia Academy 32–34
Oppenheimer, J. Robert 95

Pp

pacifism 26, 29, 67–68, 92, 95
particles 43–44
patent clerks 31–32, 42, 48, 50–52
Petersschule, Munich 18–20
photoelectric effect 65
photons 43
Planck, Max 55–57
Podolsky, Boris 86
Prague 53
Princeton, New Jersey 64, 79, 82–83, 89–90
Prussian Academy of Sciences 55, 79

Qq

quantum mechanics 56, 86, 103

Rr

racism 88–91
relativity, theory of 48–49, 55, 59–61, 66
religion 11–12, 71–72
Roosevelt, Franklin D. 93, 94, 96, 97
Rosen, Nathan 86

Ss

sailing 106–107
schools 16, 18–31
scientific papers 34–35, 39, 42–45
segregation 89–90
socks 21
Solovine, Maurice 33–34
space and time 44
speed of light 47
stars 59–61
sun 59–61
Szilard, Leo 93–94, 97, 99

Tt

Tagore, Rabindranath 73
Theory of Everything 85, 103
Theory of Special Relativity 45, 48–49

thermodynamics 39, 54
time and space 44
toys 15
Truman, Harry S. 96, 104

Uu

Ulm, Germany 9
unified field theory (UFT) 85, 103
United Nations (UN) 100
universe 69–71
University of Berlin 55–57
University of Bern 51–52
University of Zurich 52–53
uranium 94

Vv

Versailles, Treaty of 75, 76
violins 27, 102–103

Ww

warfare 29, 67, 92
waves 43
Weizmann, Chaim 104
Winteler, Jost 24
World War I 58–59, 63, 67, 70, 74, 76
World War II 47, 92–93, 96–97, 103–104

Zz

Zurich 30, 42, 52–53, 57
Zurich Polytechnic 23, 24–28, 30–31, 36, 42, 53, 54

Acknowledgments

DK would like to thank: Jolyon Goddard for additional editorial assistance; Romi Chakraborty and Pallavi Narain for design support; Jacqueline Hornberger for proofreading; Hilary Bird for the index; Emily Kimball and Nishani Reed for legal advice; Eve Mandel for her expertise on Albert's life; Jose Lazar Vargas for physics help; Stephanie Laird for literacy consulting; and Noah Harley for serving as our "Kid Editor."

The publisher would like to thank the following for their kind permission to reproduce their photographs:
(Key: a-above; b-below/bottom; c-center; f-far; l-left; r-right; t-top)

6 **Dreamstime.com:** Johan Mollerberg / A40757 (cl). **Getty Images:** Photo 12 / Universal Images Group (cra). 9 **Alamy Stock Photo:** Keystone Pictures USA (clb, crb). 17 **Getty Images:** Photo 12 / Universal Images Group. 24 **Alamy Stock Photo:** UtCon Collection. 33 **Alamy Stock Photo:** The History Collection. 36 **Alamy Stock Photo:** Granger Historical Picture Archive. 37 **Alamy Stock Photo:** Granger Historical Picture Archive. 40 **akg-images.** 41 **Courtesy AIP Emilio Segrè Visual Archives:** Besso Family. 42 **Alamy Stock Photo:** World History Archive. 43 **123RF.com:** mrtwister. 52 **Getty Images:** Brigitte BlSttler / Moment Mobile. 54 **Alamy Stock Photo:** Historic Collection. 56 **Getty Images:** ullstein bild Dtl.. 58 **Dorling Kindersley:** Gary Ombler / Brooklands Museum. 61 **NASA:** (cb). 62 **Getty Images:** ullstein bild Dtl.. 64 **Alamy Stock Photo:** Pictorial Press Ltd. 65 **Library of Congress, Washington, D.C.:** LC-DIG-hec-31006. 66 **Dreamstime.com:** Johan Mollerberg / A40757 (crb). 69 **Bridgeman Images:** © SZ Photo / Scherl. 71 **Getty Images:** Margaret Bourke-White / Time & Life Pictures. 73 **Alamy Stock Photo:** Archive PL (cra). **Getty Images:** Bettmann (cb); ullstein bild Dtl. (cla). 75 **Bridgeman Images:** © SZ Photo / Scherl. 76 **Getty Images:** Hugo Jaeger / The LIFE Picture Collection (clb); NurPhoto (cra). 78 **Getty Images:** MICHAEL URBAN / AFP. 79 **Alamy Stock Photo:** EQRoy. 80 **Getty Images:** Bettmann. 83 **Getty Images:** Oliver Morris. 86 **Getty Images:** ullstein bild Dtl.. 87 **Bridgeman Images:** © SZ Photo / Scherl. 90 **Library of Congress, Washington, D.C.:** LC-USZ62-105575. 91 **Getty Images:** Kingford P. James / Library of Congress / Corbis / VCG. 93 **Getty Images:** Wallace Kirkland / The LIFE Picture Collection (cra); Time Life Pictures / Us Air Force / The LIFE Picture Collection (b). 95 **Getty Images:** Bettmann. 96 **Getty Images:** U S Signal Corps / PhotoQuest. 97 **Alamy Stock Photo:** World History Archive. 99 **Getty Images:** Bettmann. 102 **Getty Images:** Hansel Mieth / The LIFE Picture Collection. 104 **Getty Images:** Education Images / UIG. 105 **Getty Images:** ullstein bild. 109 **Getty Images:** Bettmann. 111 **Getty Images:** ullstein bild Dtl. (cla)

Cover images: *Front and Spine:* **Science Photo Library:** US LIBRARY OF CONGRESS

All other images © Dorling Kindersley
For further information see: www.dkimages.com

ANSWERS TO THE QUIZ ON PAGES 116–117

1. Pauline and Hermann; 2. the "Dopey One"; 3. Petersschule; 4. his mother, Pauline; 5. the Olympia Academy; 6. four papers; 7. $E=mc^2$; 8. a red rose; 9. England; 10. Princeton, New Jersey; 11. the Manhattan Project; 12. Mozart and Bach